Suggestions for Leading a Study of *The Truth About God*

The Truth About God is a conversation on the Ten Commandments. It is designed to help us better understand the Ten Commandments and how they apply to Christian life. This leader's guide is intended to assist you in facilitating a discussion group so that the experience is beneficial for both you and your group.

As a discussion leader you will have the opportunity to help others obtain the answers they are seeking on their spiritual journey. The conversations in your group may cover a variety of topics as together you ask questions and seek answers. Here are some thoughts on how you can help your group:

1. Distribute the book to participants before your first group meeting and request that they come having read the first chapter. Encourage them to also read the introduction as a background. You may want to limit the size of your group to increase participation.
2. Begin your sessions on time. Your participants will appreciate meetings that begin when scheduled and

end when promised. You may want to begin your first session with introductions and a brief get-acquainted time. Start each session by reviewing the summary points of the chapter for the day.

3. Select discussion questions and activities in advance. Note that the first question is usually a general question designed to get the discussion going. Feel free to change the order of the listed questions and to create your own questions. Set a specific length of time for the questions and activities.
4. Remind your participants that all questions are valid as part of the learning process. Encourage their participation in discussion by saying there are no "wrong" answers and that all input will be appreciated. Invite them to share their thoughts, personal stories, and ideas as their comfort level dictates.
5. Some questions may be more difficult to answer than others. If you ask a question and no one responds, begin the discussion by venturing an answer yourself. Then ask for comments and other answers. Remember that some questions may have multiple answers.
6. Ask the question "Why?" or "Why do you believe that?" to help continue a discussion and give it a greater depth.
7. Give everyone a chance to talk. Keep the conversation moving. Occasionally you may want to direct a question at a specific person who has been quiet. "Do you have anything to add?" is a good follow-up question to another person. If the topic of conversation gets off track, move ahead by asking the next question in your leader's guide.
8. Before moving from questions to activities, ask members if they have any questions that have not been answered. Remember that as a leader, you do not have to know all the answers. Some of the answers may come from group members. Other answers may even need a bit of research. Your job is to keep the discussion moving and to encourage participation.

9. Review the activities in advance. Select the one you like best. Feel free to modify it or to create your own activity.
10. Following the conclusion of the activity, close with a brief prayer—either the printed prayer in the leader's guide or one of your own. If your group desires, pause for individual prayer petitions.
11. Be grateful and supportive. Thank members for their ideas and participation.
12. You are not expected to be a "perfect" leader. Just do the best you can by focusing on the participants and the lesson. God will help you lead this group.
13. Enjoy your time together.

The First Commandment

You shall have no other gods before me. You shall not make for yourself an idol, whether in the form of anything that is in heaven above, or that is on the earth beneath, or that is in the water under the earth. You shall not bow down to them or worship them; for I the LORD your God am a jealous God, punishing children for the iniquity of parents, to the third and the fourth generation of those who reject me, but showing steadfast love to the thousandth generation of those who love me and keep my commandments.

(Exodus 20:3-6)

Summary

- This commandment is a call to worship.
- All commandments are constituted by this commandment.
- We are called to bend our lives toward God.

- Our idolatry is passed on as a punishment to our children.
- The good news of this commandment is God has given us his name.

Discussion Questions

1. What insights did you receive from this chapter?
2. Through this commandment what is God saying he wants from us?
3. Why is God a jealous God?
4. What are the benefits of following this commandment?
5. How is prayer a protest against idolatry?
6. How does superstition break this commandment?
7. What is the purpose of this commandment?
8. What are the costs of following this commandment?
9. What happens when we break this commandment?
10. Why is God so passionate about our obedience?
11. What causes us to get confused about who we worship?
12. Give a summary of what Luther says about this commandment.

Practical Applications/Activities

1. Make a list of modern idols that people worship.
2. Survey people about what the first commandment is and what it means.
3. Rewrite this commandment in your own words.
4. Discuss strategies that would help you keep this commandment.
5. Discuss this commandment with your family or a friend.

PRAYER: *God, we thank you for your love for us as shown in this commandment. Help us to worship you, and only you. Continue to guide us and bring us closer to you. Amen.*

The Second Commandment

You shall not make wrongful use of the name of the LORD your God, for the LORD will not acquit anyone who misuses his name. (Exodus 20:7)

Summary

- To know God's name is a gift from God.
- To be able to call God's name entails a moral obligation.
- Not taking God's name in vain means prayers must be honest.
- Blasphemy is speech that makes God part of our lies.
- This commandment means we commit to speak truthfully to God, ourselves, and to one another.

Discussion Questions

1. What new insight did you receive from this chapter?
2. Why are names more than arbitrary labels?
3. How do we rightly use God's name?
4. How do we wrongly use God's name?
5. Why did God give us his name?
6. What points does Calvin make about simplicity of speech?
7. What causes us to break this commandment?
8. Discuss examples of how Christians break this commandment in church.
9. How are we hurt by abusing God's name?
10. What are the public consequences of keeping this commandment?
11. How would you explain this commandment to a child?
12. Why is knowing God's name such a great gift to us?

Practical Applications/Activities

1. Share the meaning of your first name. Why did your parents give you that name?

2. Discuss the story of Ananias and Sapphira in Acts 5.
3. Memorize Ecclestiastes 5:2.
4. Discuss this commandment in light of current national or local events.
5. Share why you gave a specific name to a child or pet.

PRAYER: *God, we thank you for the gift of names and the gift of knowing your name. Guide our speech so we may faithfully keep this commandment. Thank you for this time together and be with us as we leave. Amen.*

The Third Commandment

Remember the sabbath day, and keep it holy. Six days you shall labor and do all your work. But the seventh day is a sabbath to the LORD your God; you shall not do any work—you, your son or your daughter, your male or female slave, your livestock, or the alien resident in your towns. For in six days the LORD made heaven and earth, the sea, and all that is in them, but rested the seventh day; therefore the LORD blessed the sabbath day and consecrated it.

(Exodus 20:8-11)

Summary

- This commandment reminds us that we were created to worship God.
- Our time is not our own. It is a gift from God.
- Sunday is a visible mark of Christians.
- Christian time is not the world's time.
- Keeping the sabbath is a sign of trust that God governs.

Discussion Questions

1. What new insights did you receive from reading this chapter?
2. How is obeying this commandment a witness to the world?
3. What is the purpose of the Sabbath day?
4. How is the Sabbath tied to Creation?
5. What activities should we participate in on Sunday?
6. Explain: God is rest.
7. What are the economic implications of this commandment?
8. Discuss the importance of rest.
9. Why is rest so important to God?
10. What does this commandment cause us to remember?
11. What can we do to make Sunday a holy day?
12. How does Sunday give us a glimpse of eternity?

Practical Applications/Activities

1. Discuss what makes it so hard to keep this commandment.
2. What occupations require work on Sunday? What work can't be avoided?
3. Discuss what makes Sundays so special for you.
4. Recall what Sundays were like for you as a child.
5. List the benefits of attending church on Sunday.

PRAYER: *God, we were created to worship you. Thank you for this special time of rest and worship that you give us each Sunday. Help us learn to rest and enjoy the many gifts you give us. Amen.*

The Fourth Commandment

Honor your father and your mother, so that your days may be long in the land that the LORD your God is giving you.
(Exodus 20:12)

Summary

- We are to obey our parents as we obey God.
- Our parents remind us that life is a gift.
- Parents are to be honored as they honor God.
- We are to love our parents as we love God.
- This commandment reminds us that we are creatures, creations of our mother and our father.

Discussion Questions

1. What new insights did you receive from this chapter?
2. Explain in your own words what this commandment means to you.
3. What does it cost to follow this commandment?
4. What are the benefits of following this commandment?
5. Why did God give us this commandment? What is the need?
6. What does it mean *to honor*?
7. What do our belly buttons make us remember?
8. Discuss: Responsibilities of parents to children.
9. Discuss: Responsibilities of children to parents.
10. What do the authors say are current threats to the family?
11. What qualities does good parenting require?
12. What are the limitations, if any, to this commandment?

Discussion Applications/Activities

1. Share a childhood memory of your mother or father.
2. Visit a nursing home.
3. Discuss how we can honor parents who are deceased.
4. Look for examples in the newspaper of how this commandment is broken.

5. Discuss how relationships change as parents and children grow older.

PRAYER: *God, we thank you for our earthly parents and all they have done for us. Help us to continue to honor them. Thank you for being our heavenly parent and for always being with us. Amen.*

The Fifth Commandment

You shall not murder. ***(Exodus 20:13)***

Summary

- All life belongs to God.
- Genesis tells us we were created to live without killing.
- This commandment is intended to free Christians from the world's violence.
- When we take a life for any reason, we put ourselves in place of God.
- By acting as if we are peaceful, we become peaceful people.

Discussion Questions

1. What new insights did you receive from this chapter?
2. How does anger fit into this commandment?
3. What virtues must we acquire to keep this commandment?
4. What benefits do we receive by keeping this commandment?
5. Explain this commandment in your own words.
6. Is this a simple commandment? Why or why not?
7. Why did God give us this commandment?
8. How can you be guilty of breaking this commandment without killing a person?

9. What is the key to keeping this commandment?
10. List some strategies for living at peace with others.
11. How should a Christian view war in light of this commandment?
12. Discuss this commandment in relation to suicide.

Practical Applications/Activities

1. Make a list of things that kill people.
2. Discuss: Does this commandment include our killing of animals for food?
3. Make a list of reasons that people kill people.
4. Discuss Calvin's observations based on this commandment.
5. Discuss how Jesus expands this commandment in Matthew 5:21-26.

PRAYER: *God, we thank you for life. Help us to cherish and protect life. Show us how to live in peace with others. Amen.*

The Sixth Commandment

You shall not commit adultery. ***(Exodus 20:14)***

Summary

- God created us for fidelity.
- This commandment gives us the chance to show the same fidelity God shows us.
- Lust is prohibited by Christ so that no one might think it possible to be innocently lustful.
- Marriage is symbiotic. It lives off of and derives power from the other commandments.
- Throughout history, God has been faithful to us even when our love has failed.

Discussion Questions

1. What new insights did you receive from reading this chapter?
2. In your own words, explain the meaning of this commandment.
3. Why is sexual conduct taken so seriously by God?
4. What are some keys to keeping this commandment?
5. How do we benefit by following this commandment?
6. What does this commandment prohibit besides adultery?
7. What does fidelity mean to you?
8. Why does our culture make this commandment so hard to keep?
9. According to the authors, why do Christians have children?
10. What does this commandment mean to those who are single?
11. According to the authors, what is required to practice adultery?
12. What commitments are required for a successful marriage?

Practical Applications/Activities

1. Investigate how other religions view adultery.
2. Make a list of the results of adultery.
3. Discuss what is needed to recover from adultery.
4. Discuss how you could break this commandment without being married.
5. Look at how television and the movies portray sex and marriage.

PRAYER: *God, we praise you for your fidelity to us. Help us to be faithful to you through this commandment as we seek to live in peace with others. Amen.*

The Seventh Commandment

You shall not steal. **(Exodus 20:15)**

Summary

- We fail to tell ourselves the truth about our wealth.
- Whatever is "ours" is only so as a gift from God.
- There will always be thieves among us.
- To not be caught up in a world of theft requires prayer.
- Lying and riches seem to work hand in hand.

Discussion Questions

1. What new insights did you receive from reading this chapter?
2. Give a summary of this commandment in your own words.
3. How did you first learn it is wrong to steal?
4. What motivates people to steal?
5. Define *theft*. Give some examples.
6. How is a thief injured by stealing?
7. Why is it so hard to determine who is a thief and who is not?
8. Can you be a thief without knowing it? Explain.
9. How are theft and lying alike?
10. Do you agree with the statement that thievery is the most common craft on earth?
11. How are theft and murder related?
12. What is the good news of this commandment?

Practical Applications/Activities

1. Have you ever had something stolen? How did it make you feel?
2. List some ways that theft can be reduced.
3. Discuss the relationship between wealth and theft.
4. Can you become wealthy without stealing? Explain.
5. Make a list of occupations designed to prevent stealing.

PRAYER: *God, we thank you for all that you give us that can never be taken away. Guide our actions so we may protect the property of others and learn the true meaning of wealth. Amen.*

The Eighth Commandment

You shall not bear false witness against your neighbor.
(Exodus 20:16)

Summary

- To tell the truth requires work. Lying is easy.
- In order to praise a God of truth, we must be truthful.
- We are called by God to be witnesses to truth.
- "Love" is often a source for our lies.
- Nothing is more important for real friendship than the ability to speak the truth to one another.

Discussion Questions

1. What new insights did you receive from reading this chapter?
2. Give a summary of what this commandment means to you.
3. What risks do we take when we tell the truth?
4. What risks do we take when we lie?
5. How can we help others affirm the truth?
6. What gifts did God give us to help us speak the truth?
7. Can you think of a circumstance where you would not want to hear the truth?
8. What does it mean to be a witness?
9. What does this commandment reveal about God?
10. What is the purpose of human communication?
11. What is the father of all lies? (John 8:44)
12. Why would we rather be polite than truthful?

Practical Applications/Activities

1. Discuss how it feels to be caught in a lie.
2. Make a list of famous lies throughout history.
3. How does it feel when you discover someone has lied to you?
4. List some examples of how lies can be shaped by undisciplined love.
5. List some reasons why God gave us this commandment.

PRAYER: *God, we thank you for showing us the real meaning of truth. Please guide our words and actions so we will speak the truth and serve you. May we speak truthfully to you in prayer and in worship. Amen.*

The Ninth and Tenth Commandments

You shall not covet your neighbor's house; you shall not covet your neighbor's wife, or male or female slave, or ox, or donkey, or anything that belongs to your neighbor.

(Exodus 20:17)

Summary

- The ninth and tenth commandments are all about desire.
- Only God can satisfy our large desire.
- Our problem as Christians is that we long for that which is unfulfilling.
- Our desire is boundless because it is meant to find its rest in God.
- All the commandments are connected.

Discussion Questions

1. What new insights did you receive from reading this chapter?
2. Why did the authors group these commandments together?
3. What do these commandments reveal about God?
4. In your own words give a summary of these commandments.
5. Why did God give us these two commandments?
6. In what ways does advertising create desire?
7. According to the authors, what other names do we use for greed?
8. How can the church help us keep these commandments?
9. How do these last two commandments act as a summary of the Decalogue?
10. What is meant by disordered desire?
11. Why do our endless acquisitions never satisfy us?
12. Give a past example of envy in your life. What harm did it cause?

Practical Applications/Activities

1. Using a magazine, discuss the advertisements and their appeal.
2. List practical strategies we can use to control our desires.
3. Recall and share some early childhood desires for toys.
4. List some examples of manufactured needs.
5. Discuss what you have learned from this book.

PRAYER: *God, we thank you for giving us all that we own. Help us to desire only you and to not desire our neighbor's property. Thank you for this group and for time together. Guide us as we go to continue our journey. Amen.*

THE TRUTH ABOUT GOD
LEADER'S GUIDE

This book is printed on acid-free paper.

ISBN 0-687-089565

Leader's Guide prepared by John D. Schroeder

99 00 01 02 03 04 05 06 07 08—10 98 7 6 5 4 3 2 1

MANUFACTURED IN THE UNITED STATES OF AMERICA